# Vocabulary

## Publishing Credits

Dona Herweck Rice, *Editor-in-Chief*; Lee Aucoin, *Creative Director*;
Robin Erickson, *Production Director;* Kristy Stark, M.A.Ed., *Senior Editor*;
James Anderson, M.S.Ed., *Editor*; Kristine Magnien, M.S.Ed., *Associate
Education Editor*; Don Tran, *Print Designer;* Corinne Burton, M.S.Ed., *Publisher*

## Shell Education

5301 Oceanus Drive
Huntington Beach, CA 92649-1030
http://www.shelleducation.com
### ISBN 978-1-4258-0673-6
© 2012 Shell Educational Publishing, Inc.

# Table of Contents

# Introduction

## Overview

This Interactive CD contains activities that facilitate vocabulary development for students. The child's first vocabulary is listening vocabulary. As the children interact with their environment, they construct and learn concepts for which words become labels. With the vocabulary activities provided, students are able to familiarize themselves with words they encounter daily and that are conceptually related to others. Students will develop great enthusiasm for words during the activities as they experiment and progress in their vocabulary skills.

## Getting Started

### Macintosh Users

1. Insert the CD-ROM into the drive.
2. When the CD icon appears on the desktop, double-click the icon to open it.
3. Choose one activity folder and double-click to open it.
4. Open the activity (Adobe Flash file) by double-clicking it.

### Windows Users

1. Insert the CD-ROM into the drive.
2. Locate the CD-ROM drive on My Computer.
3. Double-click the drive to open it.
4. Choose one activity folder and double-click to open it.
5. Open the activity (Adobe Flash file) by double-clicking it.

# Introduction *(cont.)*

. . . . . . . . . . . . . . . . . . . . . . . . . . . . . . . .

## Navigating the Activities

### How to View the Activity Directions

Directions are provided within each interactive whiteboard activity. To view the directions, touch or click the **Directions tab** at the top left of the activity. To minimize the directions, touch or click the **Directions tab** again.

### How to Use the Tool Bar

A tool bar can be accessed from within each activity. It contains all the tools needed to complete the activities. To open the tool bar, touch or click the blue square in the bottom right-hand corner of the activity. The tools include the **move tool**, **draw tool**, **drag/zoom tool**, **highlight tool**, **notebook tool**, and **eraser tool**. With the **draw** and **highlight tools**, you can change colors and size as desired.

*Note: To change the tool you are using, click on the tool you are using again to deselect it.*

### How to Reset the Activity

Once a child has completed an activity, you can reset the activity so that the child can practice again or another child can begin the activity. To reset the activity, press the right-click button and choose **Reset** from the pop-up menu. (If you are using a single-button mouse, press and hold the **CTRL** button and then select **Reset** from the pop-up menu.)

### How to Exit the Activity

To exit the activity, press the **X** button in the top right-hand corner of the activity screen.

# What Is the Weather?

## Procedures:

1. Open the *What Is the Weather?* interactive whiteboard activity file. This activity does not require the tool bar. If you need the tool bar, click on the blue square in the bottom right-hand corner to maximize it.

2. Touch or click on the **Directions tab** to reveal the directions. Read the directions aloud.

3. Have the child touch or click on the word on the screen to hear it read aloud. For example, on the first screen, touch or click on the word *snow* to hear the word read aloud.

4. Have the child touch or click on the picture that correctly matches the word. He or she may touch or click on all pictures to hear the words those pictures represent.

5. When the correct picture is selected, the word will appear.

6. When the correct picture has been matched to the word, ask the child to touch or click on the **go arrow** to move to the next screen.

7. Continue this process with the remaining screens.

# What Is the Weather? *(cont.)*

## Activity Screens

snow

rain

sun

wind

cloud

fog

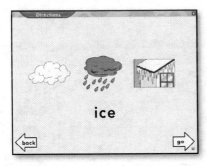
ice

rainbow

# My Favorite Things

## Procedures:

1.  Open the *My Favorite Things* interactive whiteboard activity file. This activity does not require the tool bar. If you need the tool bar, click on the blue square in the bottom right-hand corner to maximize it.

2.  Touch or click on the **Directions tab** to reveal the directions. Read the directions aloud.

3.  Have the child touch or click on the word on the screen to hear it read aloud. For example, on the first screen, touch or click on the word *me* to hear the word read aloud.

4.  Have the child touch or click on the picture that correctly matches the word. He or she may touch or click on all pictures to hear the words those pictures represent.

5.  When the correct picture is selected, the word will appear.

6.  When the correct picture has been matched to the word, ask the child to touch or click on the **go arrow** to move to the next screen.

7.  Continue this process with the remaining screens.

*#50673—Interactive Whiteboard Activities: Vocabulary*

# My Favorite Things *(cont.)*

## Activity Screens

# Places in My Community

## Procedures:

1. Open the *Places in My Community* interactive whiteboard activity file. This activity does not require the tool bar. If you need the tool bar, click on the blue square in the bottom right-hand corner to maximize it.

2. Touch or click on the **Directions tab** to reveal the directions. Read the directions aloud.

3. Have the child touch or click on the words on the screen to hear them read aloud. For example, on the first screen, touch or click on *post office* to hear it read aloud.

4. Have the child touch or click on the picture that correctly matches the word. He or she may touch or click on all pictures to hear the words those pictures represent.

5. When the correct picture is selected, the word will appear.

6. When the correct picture has been matched to the word, ask the child to touch or click on the **go arrow** to move to the next screen.

7. Continue this process with the remaining screens.

# Places in My Community *(cont.)*

## Activity Screens

post office

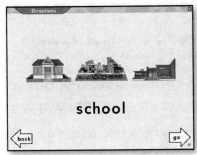

school

fire station

market

police station

park

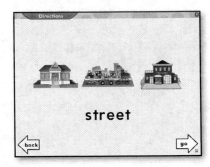

street

library

# Animal Pets

## Procedures:

1. Open the *Animal Pets* interactive whiteboard activity file. This activity does not require the tool bar. If you need the tool bar, click on the blue square in the bottom right-hand corner to maximize it.

2. Touch or click on the **Directions tab** to reveal the directions. Read the directions aloud.

3. Have the child touch or click on the word on the screen to hear it read aloud. For example, on the first screen, touch or click on the word *dog* to hear the word read aloud.

4. Have the child touch or click on the picture that correctly matches the word. He or she may touch or click on all pictures to hear the words those pictures represent.

5. When the correct picture is selected, the word will appear.

6. When the correct picture has been matched to the word, ask the child to touch or click on the **go arrow** to move to the next screen.

7. Continue this process with the remaining screens.

# Animal Pets *(cont.)*

## Activity Screens

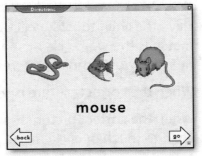

# Plant Parts

## Procedures:

1. Open the *Plant Parts* interactive whiteboard activity file. This activity does not require the tool bar. If you need the tool bar, click on the blue square in the bottom right-hand corner to maximize it.

2. Touch or click on the **Directions tab** to reveal the directions. Read the directions aloud.

3. Have the child touch or click on the word on the screen to hear it read aloud. For example, on the first screen, touch or click on the word *tree* to hear the word read aloud.

4. Have the child touch or click on the picture that correctly matches the word. He or she may touch or click on all pictures to hear the words those pictures represent.

5. When the correct picture is selected, the word will appear.

6. When the correct picture has been matched to the word, ask the child to touch or click on the **go arrow** to move to the next screen.

7. Continue this process with the remaining screens.

# Plant Parts *(cont.)*

## Activity Screens

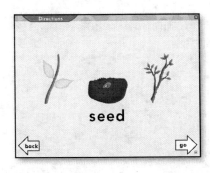

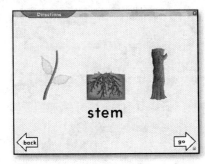

# Safety First

## Procedures:

1. Open the *Safety First* interactive whiteboard activity file. This activity does not require the tool bar. If you need the tool bar, click on the blue square in the bottom right-hand corner to maximize it.

2. Touch or click on the **Directions tab** to reveal the directions. Read the directions aloud.

3. Have the child touch or click on the word on the screen to hear it read aloud. For example, on the first screen, touch or click on the word *exercise* to hear the word read aloud.

4. Have the child touch or click on the picture that correctly matches the word. He or she may touch or click on all pictures to hear the words those pictures represent.

5. When the correct picture is selected, the word will appear.

6. When the correct picture has been matched to the word, ask the child to touch or click on the **go arrow** to move to the next screen.

7. Continue this process with the remaining screens.

## Activity Screens

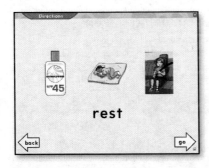

# My Family

## Procedures:

1. Open the *My Family* interactive whiteboard activity file. This activity does not require the tool bar. If you need the tool bar, click on the blue square in the bottom right-hand corner to maximize it.

2. Touch or click on the **Directions tab** to reveal the directions. Read the directions aloud.

3. Have the child touch or click on the word at the bottom of the screen to hear it read aloud. For the first screen, touch or click on the word *mother* to hear the word read aloud.

4. Have the child touch or click on the picture that correctly matches the word. The child can touch or click on each picture to hear the word that picture represents.

5. When the correct picture is selected, the word will appear.

6. When the correct picture has been matched to the word, ask the child to touch or click on the **go arrow** to move to the next screen.

7. Continue this process with the remaining screens.

# My Family *(cont.)*

## Activity Screens

# On the Go

. . . . . . . . . . . . . . . . . . . . . . . . . . . . . . . . .

## Procedures:

1. Open the *On the Go* interactive whiteboard activity file. This activity does not require the tool bar. If you need the tool bar, click on the blue square in the bottom right-hand corner to maximize it.

2. Touch or click on the **Directions tab** to reveal the directions. Read the directions aloud.

3. Have the child touch or click on the word at the bottom of the screen to hear it read aloud. For example, touch or click on the word *car* to hear the word read aloud.

4. Have the child touch or click on the picture that correctly matches the word. The child can touch or click on each picture to hear the word that picture represents.

5. When the correct picture is selected, the word will appear.

6. When the correct picture has been matched to the word, ask the child to touch or click on the **go arrow** to move to the next screen.

7. Continue this process with the remaining screens.

# On the Go *(cont.)*

## Activity Screens

car

truck

bicycle

airplane

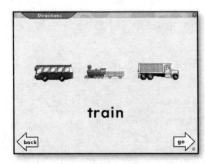

train

boat

motorcycle

bus

# Name That Shape

## Procedures:

1. Open the *Name That Shape* interactive whiteboard activity file. This activity does not require the tool bar. If you need the tool bar, click on the blue square in the bottom right-hand corner to maximize it.

2. Touch or click on the **Directions tab** to reveal the directions. Read the directions aloud.

3. Have the child touch or click on the word at the bottom of the screen to hear it read aloud. For example, touch or click on the word *circle* to hear the word read aloud.

4. Have the child touch or click on the picture that correctly matches the word. The child can touch or click on each picture to hear the word that picture represents.

5. When the correct picture is selected, the word will appear.

6. When the correct picture has been matched to the word, ask the child to touch or click on the **go arrow** to move to the next screen.

7. Continue this process with the remaining screens.

# Name That Shape *(cont.)*

## Activity Screens

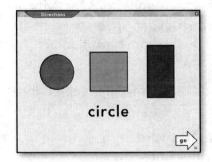

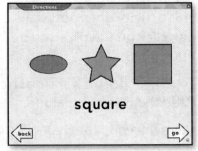

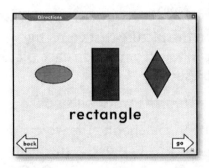

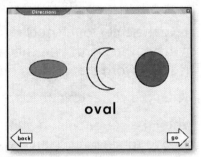

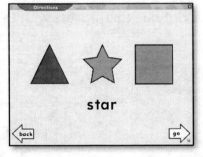

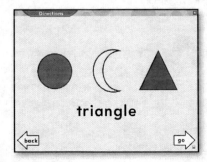

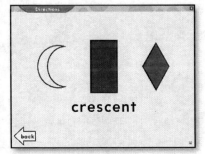

# Colorful Crayons

## Procedures:

1.  Open the *Colorful Crayons* interactive whiteboard activity file. This activity does not require the tool bar. If you need the tool bar, click on the blue square in the bottom right-hand corner to maximize it.

2.  Touch or click on the **Directions tab** to reveal the directions. Read the directions aloud.

3.  Have the child touch or click on the word at the bottom of the screen to hear it read aloud. For example, touch or click on the word *red* to hear the word read aloud.

4.  Have the child touch or click on the picture that correctly matches the word. The child can touch or click on each picture to hear the word that picture represents.

5.  When the correct picture is selected, the word will appear.

6.  When the correct picture has been matched to the word, ask the child to touch or click on the **go arrow** to move to the next screen.

7.  Continue this process with the remaining screens.

# Colorful Crayons *(cont.)*

## Activity Screens

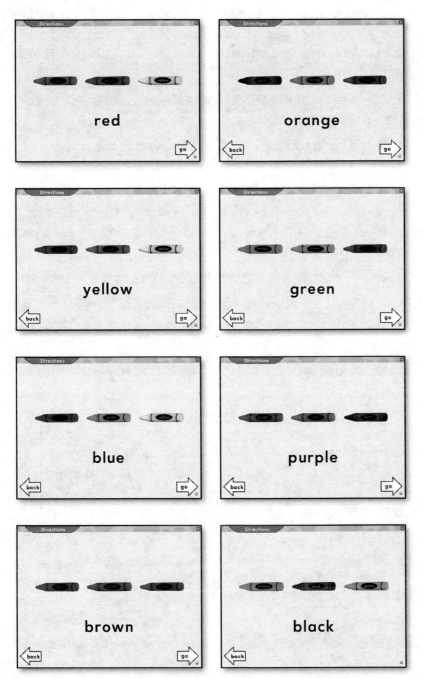

# Number Knowledge

## Procedures:

1. Open the *Number Knowledge* interactive whiteboard activity file. This activity does not require the tool bar. If you need the tool bar, click on the blue square in the bottom right-hand corner to maximize it.

2. Touch or click on the **Directions tab** to reveal the directions. Read the directions aloud.

3. Have the child touch or click on the word at the bottom of the screen to hear it read aloud. For example, touch or click on the word *one* to hear the word read aloud.

4. Have the child touch or click on the picture that correctly matches the word. The child can touch or click on each picture to hear the word that picture represents.

5. When the correct picture is selected, the word will appear.

6. When the correct picture has been matched to the word, ask the child to touch or click on the **go arrow** to move to the next screen.

7. Continue this process with the remaining screens.

# Number Knowledge *(cont.)*

## Activity Screens

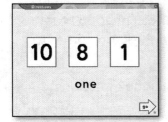

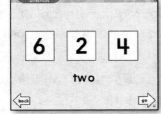

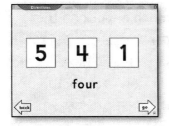

# Construction Zone

## Procedures:

1. Open the *Construction Zone* interactive whiteboard activity file. This activity does not require the tool bar. If you need the tool bar, click on the blue square in the bottom right-hand corner to maximize it.

2. Touch or click on the **Directions tab** to reveal the directions. Read the directions aloud.

3. Have the child touch or click on the word at the bottom of the screen to hear it read aloud. For example, touch or click on the word *hammer* to hear the word read aloud.

4. Have the child touch or click on the picture that correctly matches the word. The child can touch or click on each picture to hear the word that picture represents.

5. When the correct picture is selected, the word will appear.

6. When the correct picture has been matched to the word, ask the child to touch or click on the **go arrow** to move to the next screen.

7. Continue this process with the remaining screens.

*#50673—Interactive Whiteboard Activities: Vocabulary*

# Construction Zone *(cont.)*

## Activity Screens

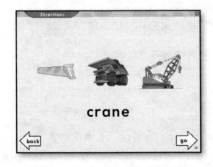

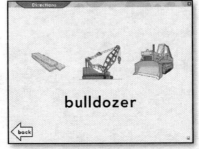

# School Time

. . . . . . . . . . . . . . . . . . . . . . . . . . . . . . . .

## Procedures:

1. Open the *School Time* interactive whiteboard activity file. This activity does not require the tool bar. If you need the tool bar, click on the blue square in the bottom right-hand corner to maximize it.

2. Touch or click on the **Directions tab** to reveal the directions. Read the directions aloud.

3. Have the child touch or click on the word at the bottom of the screen to hear it read aloud. For example, touch or click on the word *teacher* to hear the word read aloud.

4. Have the child touch or click on the picture that correctly matches the word. The child can touch or click on each picture to hear the word that picture represents.

5. When the correct picture is selected, the word will appear.

6. When the correct picture has been matched to the word, ask the child to touch or click on the **go arrow** to move to the next screen.

7. Continue this process with the remaining screens.

#50673—*Interactive Whiteboard Activities: Vocabulary*                                    ©Shell Education

# School Time *(cont.)*

## Activity Screens

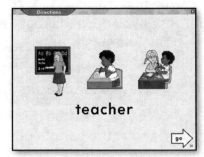

teacher

classroom

read

recess

backpack

write

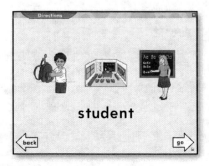

student

snack time

# My Country

## Procedures:

1. Open the *My Country* interactive whiteboard activity file. This activity does not require the tool bar. If you need the tool bar, click on the blue square in the bottom right-hand corner to maximize it.

2. Touch or click on the **Directions tab** to reveal the directions. Read the directions aloud.

3. Have the child touch or click on the word at the bottom of the screen to hear it read aloud. For example, touch or click on the word *flag* to hear the word read aloud.

4. Have the child touch or click on the picture that correctly matches the word. The child can touch or click on each picture to hear the word that picture represents.

5. When the correct picture is selected, the word will appear.

6. When the correct picture has been matched to the word, ask the child to touch or click on the **go arrow** to move to the next screen.

7. Continue this process with the remaining screens.

# My Country *(cont.)*

## Activity Screens

flag

president

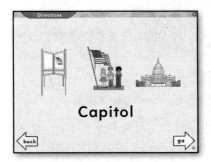

Capitol

Statue of Liberty

eagle

Pledge of Allegiance

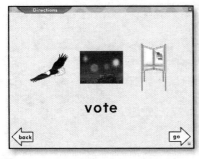

vote

Fourth of July

# My Amazing Body

## Procedures:

1. Open the *My Amazing Body* interactive whiteboard activity file. This activity does not require the tool bar. If you need the tool bar, click on the blue square in the bottom right-hand corner to maximize it.

2. Touch or click on the **Directions tab** to reveal the directions. Read the directions aloud.

3. Have the child touch or click on the word at the bottom of the screen to hear it read aloud. For example, touch or click on the word *head* to hear the word read aloud.

4. Have the child touch or click on the picture that correctly matches the word. The child can touch or click on each picture to hear the word that picture represents.

5. When the correct picture is selected, the word will appear.

6. When the correct picture has been matched to the word, ask the child to touch or click on the **go arrow** to move to the next screen.

7. Continue this process with the remaining screens.

# My Amazing Body *(cont.)*

## Activity Screens

head

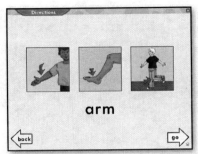

arm

hand

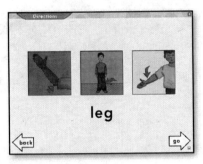

leg

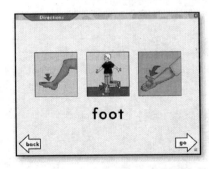

foot

knee

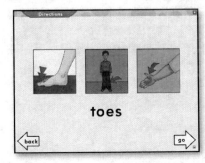

toes

elbow